HOW TO BE THE BEST IN-HOUSE LAWYER IN THE WORLD

BY

SHAHAB AHMED, Esq., MBA

ABOUT THE AUTHOR

Hello, I am Shahab Ahmed. If you are reading this page, you probably have purchased my book. Let me tell you why you should invest a few hours reading it - trust me - it is worth it. Most lawyers are mundane and boring with sad careers crunching that contract - you don't want to be one of those - do you? In this book, I have put my 20 years of experience in rising through the lowly ranks to become Chief Legal Officer and live an exciting and fulfilled life (professionally). That's why you should read it - even if you get two lessons out of it - trust me that will differentiate you from most of your colleagues and help you rise up the chain.

I am probably the most un-orthodox General Counsel in the industry with a unique personal, academic and professional journey that has given me perspective which is difficult to find in the legal world. In legal terms, I have managed multi-billion dollar commercial agreements, presided over 10s of M&As around the world, have litigated business and white collar crime cases around the world and have implemented compliance programs globally including under Department of Justice consent decrees, GDPR and CCPA. After 20 years of legal work with companies like Microsoft,

Chewy, Etihad Airways and Binary Holdings, there is no area of law I have not practiced. I am thankful and feel blessed to have the opportunities to live and work in the most exciting places in the world (Seattle, Miami, Brussels, Dubai and Bangkok). And guess what - unlike most people - I don't get Sunday blues but I love what I do everyday. I have managed (half skill, half luck) to make the GC job exciting and thrilling.

I wanted to write this book to share my experiences and help our fellow attorneys or non-attorney's who deal with legal, regulatory and compliance work for corporations. This book is designed for in-house counsels, would be in-house counsels, compliance professionals and business leaders who want to learn a thing or two about the practice of law within a company.

So now, I will tell you why my perspective is unique. I graduated with a bachelor's degree in Management Information Systems and worked for a few years as a software developer. I hated it - because I am a big picture guy and I didn't like the small box that most software programmers (at least the junior ones) live in professionally. I decided to change my profession and finished my MBA. I was recruited by Big 4 and became a management consultant. My job was to help Fortune 500 companies like Ford, Wells Fargo, General Electric in helping do M&A and manage regulatory issues. I loved the intersection of business and risk but missed the intellectual challenge because as a consultant, I was always an outsider - a hired gun going from gig to gig. I followed through with a JD (law) degree and then started working at Microsoft at the time when Microsoft was dealing with the world famous antitrust cases in the EU and US. Now that was exciting - in a sick way.

My job was to work with different business divisions like Windows, Office and others to help open API's for competitors as part of the consent decree that Microsoft entered into with the US Department of Justice. This provided me with a depth of knowledge on technology and legal issues that global corporations face across the globe. After a few years of doing this detailed oriented job, I took up a regulatory policy role which was based in Brussels. Now, I loved this job because it gave me a picture view of politics and regulations. I worked with regulators across the US, EU, Asia and Middle East Africa on legal issues such as data privacy and intellectual Property. I met senators, presidents of countries and commissioners of all the major regulators across the world. This role gave me a truly global perspective as it allowed me to work and live in DC, Brussels and Dubai. After finishing up this role, I came back to Redmond where I focused on privacy and cybersecurity on products like Office 365, Azure, Bing and Windows. Again, I was getting restless.

In 2014, one of my contacts called me up from Dubai and shared an opportunity to help build one of the largest airline loyalty programs in the world by merging seven different airlines in the world across the Middle East, Africa, Europe and India. We as a family packed-up our bags and left for Dubai and lived there for eight years. In my role as group General Counsel for loyalty group, I did M&A transactions, managed contentious board issues, drove large commercial agreements, managed 2 billion EUR commercial litigation, helped our executive team in white collar crime cases, led bankruptcy litigation around the world and managed a team that lived in Dubai, Rome, Serbia, Seychelles and India. This is the role which truly shaped my values as General counsel and taught me how important it is to have a GC which knows the business inside out and can go toe to toe with any other executive on business issues, while at the same time managing risk for the company.

Towards the end of Covid, when the airline industry was suffering and shrinking, I decided to switch back to the US and joined Chewy, the largest online pet e-commerce business in the US as GC for the e-commerce division, driving almost 10 billion dollars annually in revenue. I helped implement an efficient commercial contracting process, helped expand Chewy to China and Canada, drove SEC and CCPA compliance, helped launch Chewy's fintech business and managed a team of commercial transactions, FDA, IP and

Privacy/cybersecurity lawyers. I was having a lot of fun at Chewy but I was missing the international element since Chewy is essentially a North American business with a supply chain based in Asia.

One of my contacts reached out to me for the role of Group GC for Binary Holdings, an up and coming tech and web3 company based in Dubai, but with its SLT sitting in Bangkok. This was an opportunity to help build the team from scratch, help grow the company globally and take it to IPO. Since I have joined Binary, we have expanded across APAC, Middle East, Africa and we are expanding in Europe as we speak with a goal to expand into US and Latin American markets by 2026. This has been an incredible journey to learn a new business, hand select an amazing legal team, drive growth, open new markets, deal with regulatory ambiguity around crypto and help with the IPO process.

As you can read, my journey has been incredibly diverse and rewarding personally and professionally. I feel blessed that I always find myself with door openings at the most exciting opportunities. I have learned so many things over the years by doing them hands-on, by making mistakes, learning from such mistakes and then recalibrating my brand and approach to align with what SLT of a corporation needs and wants.

I don't like to pontificate - I like to act. That's why I have designed this book to be a practical guide based on hands-on lessons learned. You will notice certain topics and themes are repeated again and again - it's intentional to drive home key points. This is a book to teach the "approach" and not dive into details of the law. Details of the law can be researched and learned - it's the approach and mindset that I find most critical for success.

I hope you enjoy reading this book and learn a thing or two to help drive your career forward.

I dedicate this book to my amazing daughters Layla and Daniya who bring me joy everyday. They negotiate hard with me on pretty much everything. And, I am happy to lose any negotiation to them.

Table of Contents

Chapter 1: The General Counsel Glow-Up: From Risk Manager to Business Guru 1

Chapter 2: How to Be the GC Every CEO wants - your brand! 8

Chapter 3: Strategies to Supercharge Your E-Commerce Growth as GC 13

Chapter 4: Strategies to survive as a crypto GC 19

Chapter 5: How to Build a Legal and Corporate Affairs Team for High-Growth Tech Companies 24

Chapter 6: Commercial Contracts—The Necessary Evil You Can Actually Master 29

Chapter 7: IP Strategy for Tech Companies — Or, How to Stop Burning Cash on Patents You'll Never Use 36

Chapter 8: Privacy and Cybersecurity—Without Killing the Business 44

Chapter 9: Why Most M&A Deals Are Dumpster Fires — And How Not to Light the Match 50

Chapter 10: Surviving the Legal Trenches – Disputes and Litigation Without Losing Your Mind 56

Chapter 11: How to Get the Most Bang for Your Legal Buck (a.k.a. ROI on Outside Counsel) 63

Chapter 12: How to Manage the Pesky HR Issues 71

Chapter 13: The GC's Guide to Surviving (and Thriving in) the C-Suite Jungle 77

Chapter 1

The General Counsel Glow-Up: From Risk Manager to Business Guru

I've been around the block—big companies like Microsoft and Chewy, scrappy startups that grew big like The Binary Holdings, Government owned large companies like Etihad Airways, the whole corporate jungle. I have been based in the EU, the US, Middle East and Asia Pacific. I have tackled commercial contracts, regulatory issues, litigation and public affairs. And if there's one thing I've noticed and have experienced, it's that General Counsels (GCs) come in two distinct flavors.

First, you've got the old-school GC. You know the type— borning, quiet, almost no social skills, got the job because they spent years grinding through the legal trenches, giving watertight advice, running a tight risk averse (and low cost) legal department, and keeping their heads down. Their biggest win? Minimizing risk and making sure no one accidentally burns the company to the ground. And survive the SLT meetings. That's cute. But let's be real—times have changed. Unless you work for the local utilities company that has a monopoly over providing water, legal work has evolved.

These days, high growth companies don't just want a lawyer; they want a strategic powerhouse. Enter the new-age GC: part lawyer, part business whisperer, part corporate gladiator, flamboyant and vocal. Most CEOs aren't looking for someone to sit in the corner, quietly reviewing contracts—they want a consigliere, a partner in crime (minus the actual crime, of course). They want someone who can fuel growth, break into new markets, strategically get around regulations without breaking the law and drive revenue. In other words, they want a business leader first, a lawyer second.

That's a mindset shift that leaves some of the old-school GCs clutching their "briefcases" in horror. Because let's be honest—most lawyers love rules because they are generally boring and risk averse people. Business leaders? They love breaking rules (or at least bending them creatively). The trick is finding the balance: knowing when to worry about compliance with the law and when to use it as a strategic weapon.

And let me tell you, no one—not even the CFO—has a better 360-degree view of a company than the GC. While other execs are deep in their silos (Sales obsessed with quotas, Product dreaming up the next big thing, HR figuring out why people keep quitting), we're everywhere. In a single day, we're in board meetings navigating power plays, negotiating million-dollar deals, diffusing interdepartmental wars, and crafting regulatory strategies that won't land the company in hot water. Basically, we're corporate chameleons.

The best GCs don't just survive in this chaos—they thrive and they love it. I know I love the daily drama! They use their unique position to add value beyond legalese, becoming the go-to advisor for the CEO and the board. And guess what? Those are the GCs who end up with real influence (and lots of money), not just a fancy title.

The Business-First Mindset: How to Make the Shift

If you are a law firm lawyer, trying to make it in-house, read this carefully. If you are an in-house lawyer crunching through contracts or sleeping with those COSO compliance frameworks, read this even more carefully. How do you go from risk-averse lawyer to strategic GC? Here's the deal—it's all about mindset.

It starts with recognizing that your role is no longer just about keeping the company out of trouble. It's about actively driving its success. That means:

1. **Speaking the Language of Business**

If you can't read a balance sheet, learn. If you don't know what a P&L statement is, fix that. If you can't spit out your company's core KPIs, you are dead. If you can't speak to your tech guy in his language - he will get you in trouble. CEOs don't care about legal nuances—they care about growth, profitability, and competitive advantage. The best GCs understand how legal strategy ties into business objectives and can translate complex legal risks into commercial opportunities.

2. **Stepping Into the Boardroom with Confidence**

You're not just a spectator and note taker at board meetings—you're a key player. That means having a voice, offering strategic insights, and sometimes pushing back when necessary. A GC who is too timid to challenge bad business decisions is just a highly paid note-taker. And guess what? Nobody wants a note-taker who makes half a million dollars and more a year!

3. **Being Proactive, Not Just Reactive**

Traditional lawyers wait for problems to land on their desks. Great GCs anticipate them before they happen. That means building relationships with key stakeholders, staying ahead of regulatory changes, and constantly thinking about how legal strategy can drive business objectives. If you are going to wait for business to ask your advice, you will miss 80% of the issues because for business, legal is the last department they want to speak to. This means you need to immerse yourself in sales meetings, product roadmap, concept discussions, marketing strategy meetings and discussions on operational KPIs so you actually know what is going on and can shape the direction.

4. **Building a Power Network**

The best GCs aren't lone wolves. They cultivate strong relationships with external counsel, regulators, investors, and key players across the company. Trust me, having a strong relationship with your CFO, CMO and other C Suite members, you yield dividends that you won't believe. The more connections you have, the more influence you wield. So don't hide in that corner office - get out there, get drunk with the sales guy, eat pizza with the developers, attend that gala event with your CFO and CEO - it's not added work - it's the core of your job.

5. **Balancing Risk with Opportunity**

The old-school GC sees risk as something to be avoided at all costs. The modern GC sees risk as something to be managed smartly. Every big business move comes with risks, but the best leaders know how to assess them, mitigate them as much as possible, and—when the reward is worth it—take them.

Tech Company GCs: A Whole Different Ball Game

If you think the average GC has to be a business strategist, the tech company GC has to be a business strategist on steroids. The speed of change in technology dwarfs most other industries. SaaS, AI, blockchain, quantum computing—these aren't just buzzwords; they're rapidly evolving sectors with regulatory frameworks that are either brand new or don't even exist yet.

That means the tech GC needs more than just legal expertise; they need deep business and technical acumen. They have to anticipate how emerging regulations and geo political movements might impact product development, work closely with engineers to understand how technology works (because trust me, the regulators often don't), and find ways to mitigate risk when the rulebook is still being written.

A tech GC has to be comfortable in ambiguity, making judgment calls based on principles rather than clear-cut laws. They also need to be the bridge between legal, compliance, and product teams, ensuring that innovation doesn't get smothered by excessive caution while also protecting the company from legal landmines.

The Future of the GC: Evolution or Extinction

As businesses grow more complex and competition intensifies, the old ways of being a GC will become increasingly extinct. The companies that thrive will be the ones where the GC isn't just protecting the business—they're helping it grow.

The new GC, armed with legal and analytical rigor and empowered with business and organizational navigational skills, is quickly becoming the new normal. The days of hiding behind the legal department are over. Today's GC is on the front lines, shaping strategy, driving revenue, and making a real impact on the company's future.

So if you're still playing it safe, here's my advice: Step up, speak up, show up and start thinking like a business leader. Because in this game, only the bold survive.

Chapter 2

How to Be the GC Every CEO wants - your brand!

If you've made it to the general counsel role, congratulations—you're now the designated adult in a room full of ambitious, risk-loving executives who think legal is just a speed bump on their highway to success. Your job? To prove them wrong. You're not a roadblock; you're the GPS that allows them to go right up to the edge of the cliff but keeps them from driving off a cliff.

So, how do you make sure the CEO and C-suite actually want you around instead of treating you like a necessary evil? Here's your playbook.

1. Be the Lawyer Who Says "Yes"

Nobody likes a naysayer, especially not a CEO who just had a billion-dollar idea while taking a shower in the morning. If your default response is "No, we can't do that," you'll soon find yourself out of the loop until it's time to clean up a disaster. Instead, channel your inner improv actor: "Yes, and here's how we engineer this to avoid triggering a regulatory meltdown." Your job is to guide the business forward, not shut it down.

2. Speak CEO, Not Legalese

Legal jargon is great when you're talking to other lawyers, but the moment you start dropping "force majeure" and "indemnification clauses" in a board meeting, you've lost your audience. CEOs don't care about the nitty-gritty of law; they care about material risk, cost, and speed. Simplify. "This deal is risky, but if we structure it this way, we minimize exposure and still win since the up-side is more than the down-side." Boom. Now they're listening. This can be a little difficult for lawyers who were English and history majors and ended up going to law school to get a higher paying job because they think sounding pompous gives them gravitas - absolutely wrong. Sounding pompous only alienates your colleagues - stop it!

3. Make Friends Before You Need Them

Your legal team might report to you, but your real influence comes from your relationships across the company. If the only time the head of sales hears from you is when you're killing their dream contract, you're doing it wrong. Get out of your office. Have coffee with product managers. Chat up finance. East pizza with developers. Get drunk with the marketing team. Get it? Be the person they want to talk to before they do something risky, not after.

4. Know the Business Better Than the Business Knows Itself

The best GCs aren't just legal experts; they're business partners. If you don't understand how your company makes money, you're playing defense instead of offense. Learn the business model inside and out. Know what keeps the CEO up at night. When you can frame legal advice in terms of growth, revenue, and competitive advantage, you stop being a roadblock and start being a strategic weapon.

5. Be Decisive (Because No One Likes a Waffler)

Indecision is the fastest way to lose credibility. The C-suite doesn't want a 20-page memo outlining every possible risk scenario—they want a clear answer. If you're constantly hedging—"Well, it depends..."—they'll stop asking for your opinion. Make the call. Own it. If you're wrong, adjust. But at least be confident about it.Don't worry too much about your job. Do you know how many people get fired or made redundant every year? If it is meant to happen, it will happen - don't obsess over the paycheck.

6. Build a Brand and Bring the Energy

Most ih-house lawyers are boring. There, I said it. But you don't have to be. If you want to stand out as a GC, you need to be more than just the rulebook—you need to be a personality. Be exciting. Laugh. Crack jokes. Break (some) rules. Dance at the company party. Enjoy the work, and let people see that you do. When people like being around you, they'll listen to what you have to say. Your brand is not just "the lawyer"—it's "the person who makes things happen and has a damn good time doing it." I had a CEO once tell me, "wow - a lawyer with personality - that's a first" and then said, " sometimes too much personality". Now that's an ultimate complement - as far as I am concerned and it means I have changed the perception.

Final Thought: Be the GC Who Gets Invited to Happy Hour

The real secret to being the GC every CEO wants? Don't be boring. Be someone they enjoy working with. The best legal advice in the world doesn't matter if no one wants to hear it. So crack a joke, have a personality, and make yourself indispensable—not just as a lawyer, but as a trusted, strategic partner and better yet a friend that the CEO and board trusts.

Because at the end of the day, being a great GC isn't just about knowing the law—it's about knowing how to make yourself invaluable.

Chapter 3
Strategies to Supercharge Your E-Commerce Growth as GC

Being a General Counsel is like being the goalie in a penalty shootout—non-stop action, high stakes, and plenty of moments where you question your life choices. But amidst the daily legal fire drills, don't forget your bigger mission: helping the business thrive. So, let's talk about five legal strategies that will make you a hero in the boardroom (and maybe even get you a thank-you email from the CFO—hey, we can dream!).

1. Corporate Restructure: Because Taxes Are Optional (Kinda)

Not all tax jurisdictions are created equal. Some are friendly, some are downright punishing, and some make you feel like you're being mugged in broad daylight. If your company operates across multiple countries, a little bit of tax engineering can go a long way.

- Pick jurisdictions that offer favorable corporate tax rates, GST, or VAT structures.
- Don't let tax planning be an afterthought—plan it before you scale.
- Consult the right tax advisors so you're optimizing, not evading (nobody wants an unexpected dawn raid by the tax police).

A well-structured tax plan isn't just smart—it's essential for your bottom line. And hey, if you manage to shave off a few million in unnecessary taxes, expect a Christmas card from the CFO this year.

2. Supply Chain Management: Get Vendors to Finance Your Business

Here's a tip: the best financing isn't from a bank—it's from your vendors.

- Negotiate payment terms that align with your sales cycle. The goal? Pay vendors *after* you've sold the goods, not before.
- Push for extended payment terms (60-90 days if you can get it). This turns your supply chain into an interest-free loan.
- Avoid paying hefty interest to banks when vendors can essentially bankroll your inventory.

If done right, your suppliers are financing your operations, while your customers are paying you upfront. That's what we call a beautiful positive cash flow model.

3. IT Expenses: Cloud and AI are Your Friend, Long-Term IT Contracts are Not

IT people will tell you every system has a killer ROI. They're lying (or at least overly optimistic). Keep these rules in mind:

- Go cloud-based so you can scale as needed—why pay for excess capacity you won't use?
- Implement AI and automate to reduce mundane work and RIF those workers whose jobs can be eliminated without negative impact.
- Use offshore vendors for cost efficiency, but lock them down with detailed SOWs (Statement of Work), deliverables and clear acceptance criteria. Make the payment conditional on acceptance.
- Never, ever sign long-term IT agreements without a termination-for-convenience clause. If the vendor balks, remind them that competitors are just a phone call away. Sure, you can't do this with Microsoft or AWS but you can do this with 90% of the vendors.

- Big Tech will try to intimidate you in negotiations—stand your ground. They always cave eventually.

IT costs can spiral out of control fast. Your job? Keep them on a leash and ensure the company pays for what it actually *needs*, not what some overly enthusiastic IT team *wants*.

4. Shipping Costs: The Silent Profit Killer

Shipping costs can quietly eat away at your margins faster than you can say "overnight delivery."

- Either pass the cost to customers or negotiate *hard* with shipping vendors.
- Never give all your business to one shipping provider—diversification gives you leverage.
- Future-proof your merchandising and logistics for international expansion (because sooner or later, you *will* go global).

Locking into a single shipping provider is like putting all your chips on one number in roulette—risky and rarely rewarding. Always keep your options open and your contracts negotiable.

5. Data is King: Own It, Monetize It, Protect It

In e-commerce, data isn't just valuable—it's your life for retention, upsell/cross sell and acquisition of new customers. The more you control, the less you'll spend on customer acquisition and retention.

- Ensure your Terms & Conditions and Privacy Policy give you the broadest possible rights over customer data. Privacy people will tell you - privacy is a competitive advantage - they don't know what they are talking about - data is your competitive advantage.
- Future-proof for new products, services, and markets.
- Make sure your ad-tech agreements are tight—especially around targeting and retargeting. One regulatory slip-up can mean millions in fines.
- Implement loyalty programs—repeat customers are the easiest revenue stream.

Broad data rights mean lower marketing costs, better targeting, and happier stakeholders. The key? Making sure your legal agreements lock in those rights upfront.

The Bottom Line

Being a GC isn't just about playing defense—it's about being a strategic asset to the business. These five strategies won't just keep your company legally protected; they'll make you an invaluable player in the growth game. And who knows? Maybe—just maybe—you'll get that well-deserved nod of appreciation from the C-Suite. Or at the very least, a slightly less painful budget review meeting.

Now go forth and make that legal magic happen.

Chapter 4

Strategies to survive as a crypto GC

Congratulations! You've decided to jump headfirst into the wild, wonderful, and often absurd world of crypto law. Forget everything you learned at that Fortune 500 company because here in Web3, things move faster than a rug pull in a sketchy DeFi project. If you like clarity, predictability, and well-defined legal frameworks—well, tough luck. But if you thrive in chaos, ambiguity, and regulatory whack-a-mole, you might just have what it takes.

1. Embrace the Legal Twilight Zone

Crypto law is like trying to play chess while someone keeps moving the pieces and changing the rules mid-game. Regulators are making things up as they go, and that means you'll need to get comfortable with uncertainty. The SEC, CFTC, EU, and every other three-letter agency are in a perpetual state of "maybe this is illegal, maybe it's not." Your job? Stay informed, stay flexible, navigate smartly and always have a backup plan.

2. Think Global, Act Glocal (And Keep a Lawyer in Every Jurisdiction)

Crypto is borderless. Laws are not. One minute you're dealing with friendly tax policies in Singapore; the next, you're explaining why your Token isn't an unregistered security in the U.S. If you're not up to speed on the regulatory landscape across multiple jurisdictions, you'll find yourself in hot water faster than an over-leveraged trader in a bear market. Build a network of trusted local counsel—your future self will thank you.

3. Learn the Regulatory Alphabet Soup (Or Drown in It)

VASPs, EMIs, MiCA, SEC, CFTC—it's a legal jungle out there. Staying ahead of the ever-changing regulatory scene is non-negotiable. And don't just memorize acronyms; understand their real-world impact. The difference between a security token and a utility token could mean the difference between smooth sailing and a subpoena.

4. Be a Fortune Teller, Not Just a Lawyer

Crypto moves at breakneck speed. If you're only reacting to the law that was enacted last week, you're already behind. Your CEO doesn't want to hear what the law says today; they want to know what it'll say in six months when their latest DeFi project goes live. Get good at anticipating legal shifts, emerging business models, and the next big trend—because in Web3, if you're not thinking ahead, you're already extinct.

5. Ditch the Corporate Playbook (It's Useless Here)

If you think your experience at a Fortune 500 company is going to translate to crypto, think again. Hierarchies? Too slow. Bureaucracy? Deadweight. Crypto is all about speed, adaptability, and execution. Legal departments in Web3 are often one-person armies, so be ready to roll up your sleeves and do everything from contract negotiations to regulatory firefighting—all before lunch.

6. Fundraising Ain't What It Used to Be

Gone are the days of simple equity rounds. Now, you need to understand token sales, DAOs, DeFi lending, private lending with tokens as collateral, private equity and everything in between. Investors expect creativity, regulators expect compliance, and your finance team just expects you to "figure it out." Welcome to modern fundraising, where innovation and regulation are in a constant tug-of-war.

7. Know the Business Better Than Your CEO

To be an effective GC in crypto, you can't just be a legal expert—you need to be a business strategist, a tech nerd, and a regulatory psychic all rolled into one. But it's okay, you have a birds' eye view of everything that is going on - more in depth than your CEO. Understand tokenomics, gas fees, smart contracts, and everything else that makes crypto tick. If you can't speak the language of engineers, product managers, and investors, you're just a lawyer in a space that doesn't have time for "just lawyers."

8. Enjoy the Ride (Or At Least Hold on for Dear Life)

Web3 is chaotic, unpredictable, and absolutely exhilarating. The industry is young, the people are passionate, and the opportunities are endless. Ride that sports bike, drive that sports car, be drunk at the pool party - it's okay. There is no HR police forcing stupid policies. If you're longing for the stability of traditional law, you're in the wrong place. But if you're here for the adrenaline rush of navigating uncharted legal territory, welcome aboard.

9. Let AI Do the Boring Stuff

Why spend hours on legal research when AI tools like ChatGPT and DeepSeek can do it in seconds? Use AI to automate contracts, analyze regulations, and make your life easier. You don't need that 2 year associate to do the research - he is slow low and costs too much. AI can get you there 90% in 5 minutes. The robots aren't here to replace you (yet), but they can definitely help you work smarter and faster.

10. Be Scrappy, Be Nimble, Be Relentless

Crypto legal teams don't have unlimited budgets or massive support structures. You need to be resourceful, think outside the box, and find creative solutions to problems that didn't exist yesterday. Being a crypto GC isn't about playing it safe—it's about playing it smart.

Final Thoughts

This job isn't for the faint of heart, but it's one of the most exciting, dynamic, and rewarding gigs out there. If you're ready to embrace the chaos, keep learning, and stay ahead of the curve, you'll not only survive—you'll thrive. Now go forth and lawyer up, Web3 style.

Chapter 5

How to Build a Legal and Corporate Affairs Team for High-Growth Tech Companies

Let's be honest—tech companies live and die by their teams. Unlike airlines, manufacturing, or oil rigs, we don't have tangible assets like planes or assembly lines. What we do have are smart people, big ideas, and the ability to turn those ideas into reality (and private jets) faster than your competitors. So, if you're in charge of building a legal and corporate affairs team, congratulations—you're about to play one of the most strategic roles in the company. No pressure.

Think Like a Coach, Not a Lawyer

Building a legal team isn't about stacking the department with a bunch of compliance robots. It's about creating a high-performing sports team where every player knows their role and executes it flawlessly. Your job is to make sure the offense and defense work together without tripping over each other.

Your Offensive Players: Business-Savvy Lawyers

These are your playmakers—the ones who work directly with marketing, sales, product, and corporate teams. They're charismatic, adaptable, and can talk business lingo like they've got an MBA on the side. You need them to be fearless, willing to take calculated risks, and capable of making judgment calls on the fly without the two week research and memo writing. You want people who say "Yessss" 90% of the time.

Want to make them even better? Throw them into high-stakes business meetings and industry conferences. The more they understand the company's goals, the better they'll be at finding legal solutions that don't sound like "No, you can't do that."

Your Defensive Players: Compliance and Risk Gurus

Let's face it—some things in the legal department just aren't sexy. Financial regulations, anti-corruption laws, SEC filings—someone's got to do it. These are your risk managers, your regulatory watchdogs, the people who make sure you don't wake up to an SEC investigation.

But here's the trick: don't let them take over. If they had their way, your company would never take a single step without three months of paperwork. Instead, listen to about 30% of what they say (the part that actually aligns with your real risk profile) and politely ignore the rest. Balance is key.

Your Secret Weapons: Paralegals and Ops Staff

You think your senior lawyers run the department? Wrong. Your paralegals and ops staff are the unsung heroes who keep everything moving. They know the business inside and out, track SLAs, handle daily operations, and make sure the legal team isn't drowning in chaos.

Pro tip: Have your lead paralegal report directly to you. They'll keep things running smoother than most junior lawyers, mainly because they don't overcomplicate everything. Give them real responsibility—procurement contracts, commercial agreements—and watch them thrive.

Public Policy & Regulatory Affairs: Your Forward Scouts

Not every company invests in a policy team, but if you're scaling fast, you should. Governments love to throw regulatory curveballs, and you don't want to be caught off guard. Whether it's privacy laws, fintech regulations, or government procurement opportunities, having someone with strong industry connections can be a game-changer.

Can't afford an in-house team? No problem—join an industry association. It's a cost-effective way to stay ahead of regulatory trends, build relationships with policymakers, and avoid last-minute compliance fire drills.

Your Role: The Ultimate Playmaker

As the GC, you're not just managing lawyers—you're orchestrating a strategic advantage. Sometimes, you're an offensive coordinator, pushing business deals through the finish line. Other times, you're a defensive coach, shutting down an idea that will land the entire C-Suite in the jail (believe me it happens) risks before they explode. And occasionally, you just need to call a timeout before things get out of hand.

- Launching a new product? Lean on your offensive and policy teams.
- Expanding into a highly regulated market? Time to bring in the compliance squad but ignore 70% of what they say.
- Running into bureaucratic hurdles? That's where your policy folks shine and open doors.

Knowing when to deploy each team member will determine whether your company scales smoothly or gets stuck in legal quicksand.

The Bottom Line

A great legal team doesn't just protect the company—it accelerates growth. Get the right mix of talent, use them strategically, and always remember: you're here to enable the business, not slow it down. Now go build a team that wins.

Chapter 6

Commercial Contracts—The Necessary Evil You Can Actually Master

Let me be brutally honest—commercial contract work is the soul-sucking, coffee-guzzling, email-thread-extending beast of in-house legal. And yet, if you're a GC in a tech company, it's also your bread and butter. You can either tame the beast, or get buried under redlines, follow-ups, and the occasional "why is this taking six weeks" from Sales.

I've built legal teams from Silicon Valley to the Middle East, and no matter where you are, the complaints are always the same:

1. "Legal is too slow."
2. "Legal overcomplicates things."
3. "Legal doesn't get the business."

If you haven't heard these yet, congrats—you either just joined or nobody's brave enough to tell you. Let's fix that.

Rule #1: Stop Redlining Like It's a Law School Exam

Most commercial lawyers go to town on contracts like they're trying to win a Pulitzer for red ink. Stop. You are not paid by the comma or redline. In 90% of the cases - nobody gives a shit about a risk that is never going to materialize.

The 80/20 rule is your friend—80% of deals are boilerplate, repeatable, and mind-numbingly dull. That's the stuff you templatize, automate, and toss to junior lawyers or paralegals. Save your mental energy for the 20% of deals that actually matter and might explode if done wrong.

If your team is still negotiating force majeure like it's a Supreme Court case, it's time for an intervention.

Automate/Self-Service the Boring Stuff—Your Sanity Depends On It

Sales agreements? Sponsorship deals? Distribution contracts? Unless they're a one-in-a-million moonshot deal, they should run on rails.

Here's the plan:

- Create templates with clear, business-approved guardrails.

- Include your big legal protections (like indirect damages disclaimers and termination rights), then lock them in.
- Empower the business to self-serve. Seriously, give them checklists and pre-approved clauses. They're smarter than we give them credit for.

And for CLM tools? Most are overpriced hype. Don't let some shiny SaaS salesman sell you a $200k system when SharePoint, Google Forms, and Excel can do 80% of the job.

Be ready for some internal pushback—especially from folks whose job currently revolves around managing these low-risk contracts. Smile politely, then reassign them or re-skill them. We're here to add value, not hoard paper.

Procurement: Where Templates Go to Die

Procurement contracts are where optimism goes to be crushed.

- Big companies with leverage? You'll get laughed off the call.
- Small and mid-size firms? Sure, throw your template at them.
- Trying to get Microsoft to use *your* paper? Good luck. Pack snacks.

SaaS deals are especially tricky—every vendor thinks they're unique. Spoiler: they're not. But you'll still have to negotiate 10 different DPAs that say basically the same thing.

Templatize what you can. Train your junior lawyers and paralegals to handle the repeat stuff. Keep your senior folks focused on the strategic vendor relationships where actual money and risk live.

Data Privacy: The Great Delay Machine

GDPR, CPRA, PDPA—if there's a privacy law, someone's going to weaponize it to stall your deal.

Solution?

- Build one lean, readable DPA template.
- Stick to it.
- Establish fallback positions and move on.

Don't let privacy lawyers derail a $10M deal over hypotheticals. If you push back hard once or twice, they usually get the message.

Service Level Agreements: Speed Is Your New Religion

Here's a crazy idea: legal should be fast. Not sloppy. Not reckless. But fast.

Set SLAs for your team. Actually track how long it takes from first draft to signature. No, not how fast you reply with "noted"—how fast the deal gets done.

Measure success by outcomes, not how many redlines someone made. Lawyers who redline every sentence to "add value" are either insecure or bored. Either coach them up or coach them out.

Legal Must Speak Fluent Business

Your legal team should not just "support the business." They should *understand* the business—products, sales cycles, customer pain points, the whole enchilada.

Make sure every team has a legal POC. Embed them physically with the team they are supporting. Invite them to pipeline meetings. And for the love of contracts, quiz them. If your lawyer doesn't know the average deal size or churn rate, they're flying blind.

Also, align legal KPIs with business KPIs. If Sales is measured on close rate, don't measure Legal on redline count. That's like judging a firefighter by how many hoses they carry.

You, the GC: Focus on the Big Fish

Your time should not be spent fixing typos in a mid-tier reseller agreement.

Focus on the billion-dollar partnerships, strategic alliances, and moonshot bets. Know the commercials. Know the strategy. Be able to challenge the CRO or CBO if needed.

Also, never forget: commercial teams fall in love with deals. Your job is to be a responsible adult. While they're dreaming about growth, you're quietly preparing exit clauses, liabilities, and how to mop up when the whole thing catches fire.

That's where you earn your salary. If you don't think about bad scenario, your beloved sales team will throw you under the bus very quickly when the deal blows up "Legal approved it".

Final Thought: You're Not a Bottleneck. You're the Enabler-In-Chief.

Legal shouldn't be a wall. You should be the ramp. Automate what you can, coach who you must, and keep your eyes on what matters most.

Great GCs don't just protect the company—they help build it. So go forth, simplify, streamline, and make sure no one ever says "Legal is too slow" again.

(Okay, they'll still say it. But at least now it won't be true.)

Chapter 7

IP Strategy for Tech Companies — Or, How to Stop Burning Cash on Patents You'll Never Use

Let's talk about IP—the beloved playground of lawyers, tech bros with a god complex, and the occasional MBA who thinks filing five patents equals five points on the valuation scale.

If you're a General Counsel in a high-growth tech or e-commerce business, you already know this: intellectual property is either a gold mine or a bottomless pit where money goes to die. Your job? Be the miner, not the guy with the shovel tossing cash into the abyss.

I've had the good fortune (or masochism) of managing IP at giants like Microsoft and high-velocity disruptors like Chewy and Binary Holdings. I've seen what works, what backfires, and what just burns a hole in your legal budget for no good reason. Let's dive into how to do this right—strategically, surgically, and with a few laughs along the way.

First, Let's Kill the Patent Hype

Here's the deal: just because your company writes code doesn't mean you need to start hoarding patents. A lot of GCs fall into the trap of thinking patents = innovation = investor love. That's true *sometimes*. But mostly, it's just a glorified trophy case.

When someone at your company (usually the CTO, or worse, the enthusiastic developer) starts talking about filing "a few" patents, you need to pause and ask: *why*? What's the ROI? Are we doing something so unique that it actually merits protection? Or are we just feeling a little insecure because our competitors have flashy patent portfolios?

Patents are expensive—$20K to $25K a pop—and that's before you even calculate the hours of internal time spent arguing about claims that sound like they were written by a drunk AI. Unless you're in the business of licensing IP or fending off lawsuits from patent trolls, slow your roll.

IP Strategy Should Follow Growth Strategy. Not Ego.

Here's where I lose half the room: your IP portfolio is not a vanity metric. It's not about how many trademarks you have filed, how long your patent list is, or how many logos you've slapped ™ symbols on. It's about aligning every IP dollar to your growth plan.

That means:

- If you're expanding into new markets—think trademarks.
- Launching new products? Think copyrights and maybe trade secrets.
- Licensing tech to partners? Now patents *might* make sense.

Don't spend money protecting stuff no one's going to use, sell, or care about. And for the love of efficiency, stop filing patents just to meet some imaginary KPI. Your CTO's childhood dream of being an inventor does not qualify as a legal priority.

Think Long. Like, 3–5 Years Long.

In some countries, it takes years to get a trademark or finalize a copyright filing. If you're planning an international expansion next year, you're already behind.

Here's the game: forecast your growth—product, geography, partnerships—for the next 3 to 5 years. Then reverse-engineer your IP strategy from that. You don't need a crystal ball. You need common sense and maybe a decent conversation with your CMO and Chief Strategy Officer (assuming they haven't pivoted three times this week). In many cases, your CMO or CSO will not know the roadmap either - it's okay - you are smarter than them. Take a guess!

Not sure where to expand first? Most US tech companies hit Canada, then the EU, then Australia, then APAC, and eventually take on the Middle East and Africa when they're feeling bold. E-commerce, on the other hand, tends to expand to countries where they can still get the product on a boat and delivered before the customer's birthday.

You don't need a PhD in strategic planning. You need a whiteboard, some caffeine, and a few educated guesses. Guessing is legal. In fact, in this context, it's a best practice.

Domain Names: The $10 Investment That Saves You $50,000 Later

You know what's fun? Discovering that a blogger in rural Iowa owns your dream domain and wants $60,000 for it. Guess what's not fun? Explaining to your CEO why you didn't think to register it three years ago when it was $12.99. I once dealt with a scenario where a no name nutter grabbed on of the domain names we wanted and even though we offered 100,000 USD plus more, he refused to even respond.

Grab domain name permutations early. All of them. Dot com, dot co, dot xyz, dot yourfutureheadache. This is low-cost insurance. Don't overthink it—just do it.

Trademarks: Easy to File, Expensive to Fight

Trademarks are the most operational part of IP. If your marketing team falls in love with a product name, get ahead of it. Run the search. File early. If you don't, some guy in New Jersey will. And then you'll have to spend $30K convincing a court that you deserve the name more.

Rule of thumb: secure the name before your CMO prints 10,000 t-shirts. Unless you enjoy awkward conversations.

Copyrights: The Low-Maintenance MVP

For software companies, copyright is your quiet best friend. It protects your code, your UI, your documentation, and all the digital duct tape you call "proprietary content."

It's cheap. It's easy. And international treaties make it portable. Do it. Do it often. It's like brushing your teeth—annoying at first, but you'll thank yourself later.

Trade Secrets: Lock It Down

This one's simple:

- Use NDAs.
- Label sensitive stuff.
- Don't let engineers post prototypes on Slack.

Trade secrets only work if you treat them like secrets. You'd be surprised how many companies "protect" their crown jewels with a Google Doc set to "anyone with the link can view."

The Patent Trap: Just Because You Can, Doesn't Mean You Should

Let me say it again: don't file patents unless there's a *real* business case.

Patents don't stop trolls. They don't magically increase valuation. They won't make VCs fall in love with you. (Unless your VC used to be a patent litigator, in which case, I'm sorry.)

Unless you're Microsoft, Meta, or IBM, treat patents like high-end sushi: occasional, expensive, and only worth it if the quality is exceptional.

If someone on your team wants to file a patent, ask these questions:

- Is this invention actually unique?
- Could we license this later?
- Is this protecting revenue, or just an engineering experiment?
- Will we defend it in court if challenged?

If the answer to all four isn't a firm "yes," put the wallet away.

The Real Value of a GC in IP Strategy

Here's the kicker: a smart GC doesn't just rubber-stamp IP filings. A smart GC shapes the IP portfolio like a sculptor—chipping away everything that doesn't serve the business.

You're the person who aligns legal investments with ROI. Who asks the hard questions. Who saves the company from wasting six figures on "defensive patents" no one ever defends.

So be bold. Be strategic. Say no. And when your CTO looks shocked that you rejected a patent filing, smile and say, "I'm here to protect the business, not your legacy."

Then go file the copyright that'll actually matter in your next market launch.

Stay sharp. Stay strategic. And don't forget to buy that domain name today.

Chapter 8

Privacy and Cybersecurity—Without Killing the Business

Let's get one thing out of the way: if I had a dollar for every privacy or cybersecurity professional who lost all sense of proportion in the name of "compliance," I'd have retired to a beach in the Maldives by now. Well, I am close enough - I live in Thailand at the moment.

Listen, I get it—privacy laws are important, and cybersecurity is critical. But some folks in our profession act like the goal is to win a gold medal in the Compliance Olympics rather than, you know, *run a business*. You know the type: they get giddy every time the EU publishes a new regulation, or when some obscure data breach in Liechtenstein becomes the hot topic of the day. But as a General Counsel, my job isn't to play Privacy Police—it's to help build a company that's not only compliant (at least on the high risk stuff) but successful, scalable, and—here's a radical thought—*profitable*.

So, how do you build a global privacy and cybersecurity strategy that supports growth instead of strangling it? Let me walk you through it.

Step 1: Start with the Business Model, Not the Law Books

Every privacy strategy should start with one question: *What the hell does your company actually do?*

If you're an e-commerce or adtech company, customer data is basically your oxygen. You need it, you analyze it, you probably dream about it. If you're in enterprise SaaS, sure, data matters—but it's not life-or-death. And if you're in financial services, cybersecurity isn't a nice-to-have; it's a matter of survival.

Bottom line: don't copy-paste some GDPR checklist off the internet and call it a day. Your privacy and cybersecurity program should match your business model like skinny jeans match a hipster. Custom fit, people.

Step 2: Privacy Laws Are More Alike Than You Think

The funny thing about privacy laws around the world? They're more similar than they are different. Despite what privacy nerds would have you believe, most of these laws want the same basic things:

- A privacy notice
- A way to assess privacy risks (hello, PIA)
- Contracts and controls for data processors
- Some consent rules for marketing
- A plan for data breaches
- And yes, a little training

Yes, some countries care more about cookies than others (looking at you, EU), and some are more twitchy about data leaving the country. But don't get overwhelmed. Focus on the *core* requirements first. That's where you, as GC, need to come in, roll up your sleeves, and make sure the program doesn't end up as a tangled mess of overkill policies and bureaucracy.

Step 3: Appoint Someone Smart—Not Just a Compliance Robot

Here's a mistake I see too often: putting a pure compliance person in charge of privacy. Don't do that. Seriously, don't.

You need someone who speaks *business*, not just legalese. Someone who can walk into a room of product managers, hold their attention, and not scare the living daylights out of them with terms like "cross-border transfer mechanism" or "data minimization." In short, someone with commercial acumen, stakeholder skills, and enough personality to not be mistaken for a privacy bot.

Step 4: Risk-Based, Always

Yes, I know Djibouti has a privacy law. No, I don't think you need to make it a core part of your global strategy unless you've got 1,000,000 customers there (and if you do—wow, let's talk).

Your focus should be proportional. If you're based in North America, California is your privacy north star. In Europe, it's GDPR. In APAC, look to Singapore. MENA? Saudi and UAE. And if you're building a global program, GDPR and California together make a solid baseline.

I once helped run privacy for an airline group that flew to 131 countries. Do you think we built a privacy program for 131 countries? Hell no. That's a one-way ticket to burnout.

Step 5: Don't Fall for the "Most Stringent Law" Trap

Here's a fun analogy: following the most stringent global privacy law everywhere is like voluntarily paying the highest global tax rate, even when you don't have to. Sounds absurd, right?

Privacy zealots will tell you to go with the strictest standard "just in case." I say: don't be ridiculous. Unless the law *requires* it, don't block your business partners from doing something legal just because some other country doesn't allow it.

Of course, you've got to balance efficiency—having too many custom rules per region can be a nightmare. But when in doubt, let common sense—not paranoia—lead the way.

Step 6: Let's Talk Cybersecurity (But Let's Keep It Chill)

Cybersecurity is a different beast. It's not as heavily regulated (unless you're under SEC's cyber rules or NYDFS). But it can bite hard when it goes wrong. Ransomware, data breaches, government investigations—these are the stuff of nightmares.

As GC or CPO, you're not the CISO. You don't need to be setting firewall rules. But you *do* need governance. Are risks being identified? Mitigated? Reported to the board? Is there an incident response plan that doesn't involve panicked Slack messages at 2 AM?

Work with your CISO. Make sure there's a proper GRC (governance, risk, compliance) program in place. Threat modeling?

Yes. Tabletop exercises? Absolutely. Cyber drills are the fire drills of the digital age—do them.

Final Thoughts

Building a privacy and cybersecurity program isn't about winning awards from regulators. It's about building trust—trust with customers, regulators, and your own employees—while still giving the business room to breathe.

So go ahead, build that program. Just don't let the privacy nerds turn it into a compliance dungeon. And remember: it's not about being perfect. It's about being smart.

And if you can pull that off while keeping your company out of hot water *and* out of the headlines—well, congratulations, you're officially a badass GC.

Chapter 9

Why Most M&A Deals Are Dumpster Fires — And How Not to Light the Match

Let's get one thing out of the way up front: most M&A deals suck. Okay, maybe not right away. At first, they look all shiny and glamorous—press releases, champagne toasts, lots of smiles and headshots of executives shaking hands. But behind that corporate romance novel cover lies a cold, hard truth: 70% to 90% of M&A deals fail. That's not a typo. That's Harvard Business Review, people. I worked in a job where we had a strategy of growth by acquisition. Guess what, after 4 years, and about 5 billion dollars later, pretty much all of our acquired company went bankrupt - it's true. Our ex-big 4 and McKinsey fancy corporate development guys thought we could turn these companies around - they were absolutely wrong.

Now, here's the kicker—most of them don't fail because of legal problems. No. They fail because someone got too excited, skipped the strategic foreplay, and just jumped straight into bed with a company they didn't understand.

So where does that leave me—as the General Counsel? Right smack in the middle of the mess. And if you're a GC reading this, pull up a chair, because I'm going to tell you how not to screw it up.

Step 1: Don't Be a Deal Robot — Be a Strategic Partner

One of the biggest mistakes I see GCs make is thinking their job in M&A is just to *paper the deal*. You know, draft the SPA, tick the due diligence boxes, and call it a day. That's rookie stuff.

The real value of a GC? Understanding the "why" behind the deal. Why are we buying this company? What are we really trying to achieve? Is this a strategic fit, or are we just trying to buy our way into a market where we have no business being? Your fancy big law lawyer won't really do this - why? He doesn't really care - he just wanted to book 200-300 K USD revenue and move on to the next deal.

You've got to ask those uncomfortable, irritating, CEO-squirming questions. Channel your inner toddler and keep asking, "But why?" until people either give you real answers—or leave the room in frustration (which is also an answer, honestly).

Step 2: Play the Devil's Advocate (And Not Just Because It's Fun)

Sometimes, the best move is not to make the move at all. I've seen companies jump into acquisitions they had no business doing—when they could have licensed the IP, partnered strategically, or just… I don't know… focused on fixing their own house first?

So, ask: Is there a simpler, cheaper, less insane way to do this?

M&A is like getting married to someone after two dates because they seemed nice and had a cool job. You need to be the friend who pulls them aside and says, "Are you *sure* this is a good idea? Do they even like dogs?"

Step 3: Due Diligence with a Purpose (Not Just a Checklist)

Look, due diligence isn't sexy, but it's where the bodies are buried. And no, I don't mean metaphorically—I mean *literally* in some jurisdictions.

If you're buying a company for their IP, make sure they actually own it. If you want their customer base, check the privacy policies, consent frameworks, and whether marketing to them is even legal. If you plan to do layoffs, better check local labor laws. If there's a union involved? Get ready for fireworks. And if the acquisition is politically sensitive? Well, good luck—you're going to need it.

I always tell my team: due diligence is where you figure out if this fairy tale ends in a happily ever after or a bankruptcy court.

Step 4: Structure the Deal Like You Actually Care About the Outcome

Most M&A lawyers with five years under their belt can draft a halfway decent purchase agreement. AI will probably do it better and faster by next Thursday.

But structuring a deal that actually delivers the business objectives? That takes experience, judgment, and a **ninja-level sense of diplomacy**. Deals break down all the time—people yell, stomp out of rooms, send angry emails in all caps. Your job as GC is to hold the line on the things that matter, let go of the stuff that doesn't, and keep the train from flying off the rails.

Also, don't let the flashy ex-big 4 and J.P. Morgan guys and consultants bully you. Just because they wear expensive suits and talk fast doesn't mean they're right. If they were, 90% of deals wouldn't be a disaster.

Step 5: The Real Work Begins After the Champagne Pops

Everyone's all high-fiving and taking selfies after the deal closes—but that's when the hard part starts: integration.

Cultures clash. Systems don't talk to each other. People are confused, cranky, and convinced the other team doesn't know what they're doing (which, let's be honest, is sometimes true).

Stay involved. You need to be there, sleeves rolled up, helping to navigate the integration jungle. Because if the integration fails, the whole deal fails. Period.

Step 6: Plan for the Divorce Before the Honeymoon

Nobody wants to think about the breakup when they're falling in love with a shiny new target company. But guess what? Sometimes things fall apart. Markets crash. Revenue projections were pure fantasy. Leadership changes and suddenly, no one wants to hold hands anymore.

So as GC, you better have an exit strategy built into the deal—preferably one that doesn't torch your entire company on the way out.

Whether it's protecting IP, isolating liabilities, or preserving your ability to walk away without dragging ten years of litigation behind you, this is where you earn your keep.

Bottom line: If you're a GC and you think your role in M&A is to just keep the lawyers and bankers in line, you're thinking too small. Your job is to challenge strategy, sniff out risks, poke holes in fairy tales, and build real protections for when things go sideways.

You are not the deal killer—you're the reality check. The one who sees the potholes before the car crashes

Chapter 10

Surviving the Legal Trenches – Disputes and Litigation Without Losing Your Mind

Let's be honest: you're not really a *grown-up* General Counsel until you've stared down the barrel of a serious lawsuit and lived to tell the tale. I'm talking about the kind of drama where the C-Suite's hair is metaphorically (and sometimes literally) on fire, your inbox is a digital war zone, and your company's reputation—or entire future—is potentially on the line. If you've never had to navigate through this storm with poise and strategic precision, then you're still in legal adolescence. Sorry, I don't make the rules.

The truth is, legal leadership gets real when things get *messy*. That's where the job stops being about pristine memos and becomes about judgment, grit, and strategic guts. You don't earn those qualities reading case law in a quiet corner—you earn them in the courtroom (or more often, the boardroom), when the stakes are high and every move counts.

First Rule: Stay Cool, You're the Designated Adult

The moment a breach notice, a payment demand, or a full-on lawsuit lands on your desk, there's one critical thing you must do immediately: don't freak out. Everyone else will—especially the CEO and senior leadership. You? You're the designated calm one. The zen master. The adult in the room.

Yes, the claim might be outrageous. Yes, your company might be unfairly targeted. No, that doesn't give you permission to slam your laptop shut and scream into a pillow. Your role is to lower the temperature in the room. Tell your CEO, "I've got this," and mean it. Then, get to work.

Know Your Beast: Identify the Type of Claim

Before you do anything else, figure out what kind of monster you're dealing with. Is this an opportunistic lawsuit in a jurisdiction you've never even heard of? A terminated vendor seeking revenge? A disgruntled former employee? Or, worse yet, is it a regulator with subpoenas in one hand and press releases in the other?

Each flavor of litigation needs its own strategy. Take it from someone who's juggled contentious disputes across the U.S., Germany, the UAE, and more—I once managed a €2 billion lawsuit from a bankruptcy administrator backed by litigation funders. That kind of dispute is not a "quick settlement and go" situation. It's war. On the other hand, if you're dealing with a cookie-cutter class action with thin legal legs, you might be able to toss a few thousand dollars at it and make it disappear.

Live by the 80/20 rule: 80% of claims are noise. Settle them fast and move on. But the 20%? That's where you dig in, sharpen your tools, and get strategic.

Do Your Homework Like Your Company's Life Depends on It (Because It Might)

For anything that rises above routine, build a foundation. Start with a proper litigation hold. Then get your hands on the facts—real facts, not the "I think this happened" fluff. Assign someone smart (preferably someone who's seen daylight recently) to gather emails, contracts, internal notes—anything that paints the full picture.

And I mean *written* reports. If you're not getting documentation, you're flying blind. Use your senior counsel or outsource it to someone competent, but make sure you own the facts before you start swinging.

Also, don't be shy about getting early advice from your outside counsel—especially if there's foreign law, tricky procedural quirks, or the chance of actual jail time involved. Get the odds, the costs, the timeline, and the worst-case scenario spelled out. Then build your case file like an old-school war chest. I still use a paper file for big cases—a trick I picked up from a crusty British solicitor who wore suspenders and read contracts like poetry. Mock him if you want, but the man never lost a file or a fight.

Business First, Drama Last: Decide How You Play the Game

Litigation is business. Full stop. I don't care how angry you are or how absurd the other side's claim seems—your next steps should be based on facts, risks, and probabilities.

Ask yourself:

- Can we win?
- How much will it cost to get there?
- What's the potential payout?
- Is the other side serious or just fishing?
- Are there reputational or political grenades hidden in the details?

If the odds are bad, settle and move on. No need to drag it out to prove a point. If the stakes are huge and your case is solid, play the long game. Just don't underestimate how long or how annoying it can be. I once spent six months negotiating a settlement with a vendor CEO—back and forth with legal letters, settlement proposals, and philosophical debates about the meaning of "reasonable."

And in the rare case where your CEO and SLT are personally at risk of criminal prosecution—yeah, no brainer. You fight like hell. Been there, done that. Wasn't fun, but it was necessary.

Keep the Execs in the Loop—Without Spooking Them

Let's talk about managing up. Your CEO watches *Suits*, so they think litigation is about dramatic courtroom takedowns and emotional monologues. Your job is to manage expectations—calmly and with numbers.

Don't walk into a boardroom waving red flags. Deliver short, crisp updates—ideally a one-slide summary. Stick to facts: cost estimates, timelines, strategic options. Leave out the drama, unless it's actually useful. And try to keep the audience small—just the decision-makers. The fewer the egos in the room, the smoother your update goes.

Assemble Your A-Team and Run It Like a Project

If you're going to war, don't bring a butter knife. Get the best litigators you can afford. Bring in experts, PR consultants, investigators—whoever you need. And then run the operation like a product launch. Weekly stand-ups, clear milestones, deliverables, timelines.

If you're too busy (and let's be real, you are), delegate project management to a trusted senior counsel. But stay close enough to make key decisions and adjust strategy when needed.

Litigation isn't a sprint. It's a marathon—on a mountain—while carrying a backpack full of bricks. You'll lose steam. The team will get frustrated. Momentum will stall. That's normal. Keep pushing.

Final Thought: You're Not in This to Win Courtroom Oscars

People still think lawyers are trial warriors who live for the courtroom. Maybe litigators are. But GCs? We know that a three-year court battle over a clause in a vendor contract is not a badge of honor. It's a massive drain on your time, energy, and company focus.

Yes, you fight when it matters. But you fight smart. You fight with ROI in mind. Because at the end of the day, your job isn't to score dramatic wins in court—it's to protect the business, keep the engine running, and make sure everyone sleeps at night (even if you don't).

Chapter 11

How to Get the Most Bang for Your Legal Buck (a.k.a. ROI on Outside Counsel)

Let's talk about one of the biggest line items in your legal budget: outside counsel. Or as I like to call them, "smart humans with expensive clocks." On average, 40–50% of a US company's legal budget is spent on these folks. That's a *lot* of guacamole. And whether your budget is big, small, or somewhere between "Please help" and "Elon Musk," one universal truth remains: if you're not getting max value from that spend, you're doing it wrong.

This isn't about pinching pennies. I'm not here to tell you to squeeze your law firm until they bleed discounts (that's what old-school GCs do). The real challenge—the *modern GC challenge*—is to optimize yield from every dollar you spend. Because it's not about cost-cutting, it's about performance investing.

Here's how to turn your outside counsel spend from an expense into an ROI-generating machine.

1. Use the Ferrari Only When You Actually Need the Ferrari

Big Law (hello, Am Law 100) charges around $1,000 an hour. That's not a typo. That's *one thousand* dollars for one hour of thinking. So before you call in the legal Avengers, ask yourself: is this really worth it?

If the issue is existential—think billion-dollar litigation, regulatory disaster, or some M&A that could tank the company if it goes sideways—yes, bring in the big guns. Break out the Ferrari.

But if you're reviewing a vendor NDA or negotiating a lease renewal? Don't waste supercar money on grocery runs. A competent regional firm (a Honda, if you will) will get the job done just fine.

Lesson: Not every matter needs a Ferrari. Keep a Honda—or even a Vespa—in the garage.

2. Build a Full Garage of Legal Vehicles

You want a law firm portfolio that looks like a well-stocked garage. A Ferrari, a Honda, a Ford Ranger, and yes, a Vespa scooter.

- Ferrari = Top-tier global firm for high-stakes deals or litigation
- Honda = Solid regional firm for bread-and-butter contracts
- Ford Ranger = Practical firm that can handle tough terrain (like local labor issues or regulatory work)
- Vespa = Boutique shop or freelance counsel for quick, cheap, and cheerful tasks

Having the right vehicle for the right terrain is how you maximize efficiency and speed without blowing your entire fuel budget.

3. Billable Hours: The Never-Ending Love Story

Every law firm partner always says: "We care about the long-term relationship, not short-term billables."

Reality: It's always about the billable hours.

You know it. I know it. Even their junior associates crying into spreadsheets at 1 a.m. know it. Law firms sell one thing: human time. So your job is to control how much of it they burn on your projects.

How? Easy:

- Send them tight, focused mandates.
- Have your in-house team do the legwork—then send a pre-drafted memo or term sheet to outside counsel just for validation.
- Use ChatGPT, a paralegal, or even your own brain to draft basic T&Cs, and have the firm polish them, not build from scratch.

Box them in. Control the scope. Make it hard for them to bloat the bill. Be ruthless about defining value.

4. Are You Buying Bandwidth or Expertise?

This question is *everything*. Sometimes you're overwhelmed, and you just need more humans. Other times, you're diving into an exotic, highly technical issue (say, tax structuring in India), and you need a specific expert.

If it's just extra bandwidth for a 3+ month project, don't pay $800/hour for it. Use:

- Legal outsourcing companies or vendor lawyers in low cost countries

- Secondments
- Alternative legal service providers (ALSPs)

If you're paying for expertise, make sure you're getting the right person—not just someone with a fancy firm name and a surprisingly vague LinkedIn profile.

Pro tip: Law firms don't have expertise—lawyers do. Hire the brain, not the brand.

5. Geography Arbitrage Is Your Friend

A partner in Rome will charge 60% less than a partner in New York. The same goes for Cairo vs. Dubai, or Bangkok vs. Singapore.

So if you're dealing with regional work, ask:

- Can I get the same quality of legal work from a lower-cost jurisdiction?
- Can I use a local expert in Vietnam instead of a "Southeast Asia Practice Group" based in Hong Kong charging double?

Not only do you get cheaper rates, you often get faster response times and more localized insights. Win-win.

6. Always Get Bids. Yes, Even for Legal Work.

Legal people hate procurement. But let's get over it: you're spending company money. Just like marketing, logistics, or IT, legal should get multiple bids for major projects.

Yes, it's a bit awkward. Yes, law firms hate it. But:

- It drives down price.
- It keeps the firms sharp.
- It reminds them they're not the only game in town.

Just use discretion. If the same firm has been handling an ongoing, complex, multi-year dispute—maybe don't swap them out to save $10K. But for new or modular matters? Shop around.

7. Fire the In-House Counsel Who Outsources Everything

You know the one.

They send *every single issue* to outside counsel—no matter how basic. They love the phrase "Just to be safe…" while handing off the simplest employment clause or marketing review.

Stop the madness. Review your outside counsel spend and map it to individual in-house lawyers. If someone's consistently outsourcing low-value work, it's time for a tough conversation. If they don't shape up?

Let. Them. Go.

You're not running a relay team where everyone hands off their job to someone else. You're running a business-critical legal function. Outsourcing everything is lazy, expensive, and sets a terrible culture.

The ROI Mindset: Spend Like a GC, Not Like a Tourist

Outside counsel will always be part of your world. And that's fine. But how you *use* them is what separates a budget-burner from a legal ROI ninja.

- Know when to bring in the Ferrari—and when to call the Vespa.
- Define what you're buying: capacity or expertise.
- Trim the fat with smart scoping, offshore arbitrage, and internal prep work.
- Hold your in-house team accountable. Demand that they manage spend like it's *their* money—because ultimately, it is.

Want to go next level? Build a scorecard system to rate outside counsel quarterly. Or run a "Legal Budget Olympics" with your team. Make it a game, make it a culture.

Because being smart with outside counsel isn't just about saving money—it's about *showing the business you know how to spend it wisely.*

Let's face it: you *will* spend hundreds of thousands—maybe millions—on outside counsel.

Might as well make sure every dollar brings you a return.

Chapter 12

How to Manage the Pesky HR Issues

If you're a General Counsel (GC) at any company with more than five people and a dog, you'll eventually find yourself neck-deep in HR issues. You didn't go to law school to mediate office drama or navigate the thrilling world of employee exits, but here we are. HR issues are like that rickety air conditioning unit in the office—nobody wants to deal with it, but if you ignore it, things will get way too hot.

First things first—understand that employment law is a mess. A glorious, jurisdictionally inconsistent mess. In the U.S., we have employment-at-will, meaning someone can be fired for being terrible at their job, for wearing Crocs to work, or because their manager simply had a bad burrito. Europe, Asia, and the Middle East? Not so fast. Those are employment-by-contract jurisdictions, where employees are often treated like unicorns whose feelings must never be hurt.

So, if your company operates in more than one country, welcome to the land of complexity. Let's walk through the big hairy buckets you need to stay on top of.

Executive Compensation and Exits

Hiring executives is a lot like dating someone way out of your league. You'll promise them the moon, a golden parachute, equity that vests yesterday, and all kinds of weird clauses you barely understand. And then—surprise—they're not a great fit.

The smart GC knows to plan the break-up *before* the honeymoon. Read every clause, ask the tough questions, and imagine the worst-case scenario from Day 1. Make sure there's an exit clause that doesn't involve your company hemorrhaging cash and reputation. Don't let the executive package turn into an alimony nightmare.

Employee Exits

Now to the fun part: getting rid of people. Whether it's poor performance, policy violation, or "we just don't need that role anymore," there's a right way to do it.

- **Non-performance?** Document everything like your life depends on it. You're not micromanaging, you're building your court defense.
- **Policy violation?** Investigate, document, and make sure the process looks like a CSI episode. Drama is fine, but drama with paperwork is better.
- **Redundancy?** Build a rock-solid case. And whatever you do, don't post a job ad for the exact same position three weeks later. That's like telling someone you can't date because you need space—then proposing to their identical twin.

In the U.S., a fired employee can walk straight to a contingency-fee lawyer and file a claim. Doesn't cost them a dime. If you've done your job, you'll settle for 10-20 K USD and move on. If not, buckle up.

In places like the EU, it's even more intense. If you mess up, a judge can *reinstate* the employee. Let that sink in. They come back to work like ghosts from HR past. That's why I always tell new businesses to start with contractors in employee-friendly jurisdictions. It's a lot easier to say "we're not renewing your contract" than to fight for your life in labor court.

The Joy of Unions

If you work in tech, you might've dodged the union bullet. But get into e-commerce or manufacturing, and suddenly you're dealing with collective bargaining, picket lines, and enough acronyms to make your head spin.

The trick? Prevention. Work with HR and leadership to create an environment where employees *don't want* to unionize. Respect, fair wages, and reasonable policies go a long way. And those hourly workers? Be mindful of tricky issues like pay for changing clothes or waiting in security lines. One wrong call, and you're funding your next company barbecue through a class action settlement.

Let me tell you, dealing with airline unions in Italy and Germany was a career highlight—like getting a root canal while reading Kafka. Judges in those countries are not on your side. If you're wearing a suit and they're wearing a uniform, guess who wins? Spoiler: it's not you.

Hire professionals. Build relationships. Negotiate contracts. Pray. Repeat.

Policies: Your Best Friend and Worst Enemy

You know the list—conflicts of interest, IP ownership, anti-bribery, anti-harassment, and all the other greatest hits. But here's the thing: those policies need to make sense. I've seen policies written by well-meaning HR folks that sound like ancient scrolls. Nobody can follow a policy written in legal Klingon.

Keep it clear, practical, and enforceable. And for the love of all that is legally sound, *follow your own policies consistently*. Nothing will tank your case faster than inconsistent enforcement. If one employee gets a warning for something and another gets fired for the same thing, you just handed the opposing counsel your lunch.

Also, remember—your HR and leadership team are human. They're biased, emotional, and sometimes, just plain petty. They'll go soft on their favorites and hard on their nemeses. That creates patterns. Patterns that don't hold up in court.

So be the GC who sees everything. Be the fairness hawk. Be the paperwork ninja. Because when the HR drama lands on your desk, it's not just about solving a problem—it's about keeping your company out of the headlines and yourself out of the witness box.

Welcome to the glamorous world of HR issues. You didn't ask for it, but you're definitely in it now. Cheers!

Chapter 13

The GC's Guide to Surviving (and Thriving in) the C-Suite Jungle

Welcome to the C-suite. You're no longer just the legal eagle—you're now part consigliere, part strategist, part crisis therapist, and occasionally, the only adult in the room.

Being General Counsel at the top levels of a company isn't about quietly reviewing contracts in the shadows. Nope. It's about influencing power, navigating politics, and helping the company win without landing it in handcuffs. If you thought this job was about legal memos and risk matrices, you're in the wrong book.

Let's dive into your playbook for managing the swirling madness that is boardroom and senior leadership team dynamics—with poise, precision, and just enough caffeine to keep you sane.

Boardroom & SLT Politics: Play the Game, or Get Played

Let's be honest: executive meetings are a game of thrones—and everyone thinks they're Daenerys. But unlike the rest of the cast, you don't get to breathe fire or behead people. Your weapon of choice is *strategy with a smile.*

Stay Positive, Even If You're Internally Screaming

Legal minds are trained to spot risk—and sound the alarm. But sounding like a siren in the boardroom will get you branded as "that person who always says no."

Flip the narrative:

- Don't say, "This violates XYZ regulation."
- Say, "Here's a smarter path that gets you to the same goal without triggering a federal investigation."

Be More Than Legal

Your best move? Be the generalist with a legal toolkit. Know the business as well as your COO. Understand the market like your CMO. If your value starts and ends with "legal risk," you'll be invited to meetings after the real decisions are already made.

Build Your Inner Circle

Play favorites. You heard me. Pick a few key execs—product, finance, ops—and give them white-glove service. Respond fast. Be solution-oriented. Become the first person they call before making a move. Trust me, when the board starts asking questions, you want those people speaking up for you.

Drive Hard for Results: The GC as a Business Engine

You're not just there to keep the company out of jail. You're there to push the company forward—safely, strategically, and without becoming the person who's allergic to deadlines.

Build a Legal Team That Hustles

Hire people who understand urgency. The business doesn't stop moving just because your junior counsel wants to triple-check clause 14.3 for fun. Foster a culture where the team asks, "How can I make this happen *safely*?" not "Is this perfect?"

Fail Fast. Learn Faster.

Something didn't work? Good. Own it, fix it, and move on. If you pretend like your team is bulletproof, everyone will lose trust. Great GCs know how to fail, pivot, and come back with a better plan.

Own the 2–3 Year Horizon

Stop chasing the fire of the day. That's what junior lawyers are for. Your job is to see around corners:

- What legal challenges will come with the company's next big product?
- What regulators are going to care about your expansion into Southeast Asia?
- What contracts will turn into hand grenades 18 months from now?

Being proactive makes you look psychic. And psychic GCs get promoted.

Manage Your CEO Without Getting Fired

Your CEO is under pressure. Everyone wants their attention, and most of them are asking for budget. You, however, have a different job: be their right hand, their voice of reason, and occasionally, their escape hatch.

Be Their Consigliere, Not Their Compliance Officer

Yes, you're the legal conscience of the company. But don't just wag your finger when they want to move fast. Be the person who says, "Here's how to do that *without blowing up the company*."

Understand their priorities:

- Revenue growth
- Investor confidence
- Operational speed

Then align legal with those, not against them.

Know the KPIs of Every SLT Member

If you don't know what the head of Sales is measured on, you won't understand their urgency. If you don't know Marketing's deadlines, you'll be blindsided by a campaign that went live before you could review the T&Cs.

Be plugged into their world, or risk becoming the legal speed bump everyone tries to avoid.

Stay Ahead of the Curve

If legal is always reacting, you'll get blamed for slowing things down—even if it wasn't your fault. Build workflows that anticipate needs. Embed legal in product development. Review things *before* they become urgent. This makes you look like a genius.

Lead with Authority, Not Ego

Being GC isn't about swinging your title around. It's about leading clearly, decisively, and fairly. Here's how to lead the team—and hold your own in the C-suite.

Support Your Stars, Challenge the Slackers

Reward high performance. Praise publicly. Give your top performers big, visible projects.

But don't tolerate mediocrity. If someone on your team constantly punts decisions to outside counsel or misses deadlines, call it out. One bad apple in legal can rot your reputation across the whole company.

Take Feedback, Not the Fall

C-Suite meetings are a political minefield. When something goes wrong, someone will try to blame legal. Be ready:

- Know the facts.
- Document decisions.
- Speak calmly, but firmly.

Own what's yours—but don't become the company's scapegoat.

Say Yes (Strategically)

The company wants fast approvals. Your job is to say "yes," with guardrails:

- Yes, we can launch the campaign—if we adjust the claims.
- Yes, we can sign this agreement—if we add this clause.
- Yes, we can go public—after we fix the 13 gaps in compliance.

"Legal said no" is a reputation killer. Be the GC who finds paths, not walls.

Conclusion: The GC as a Business Leader (Disguised as a Lawyer)

Let's get one thing straight: you're not just the lawyer in the C-suite. You're a full-blown business executive who happens to speak fluent "legal."

You:

- Shape business strategy
- Manage power dynamics
- Anticipate threats
- Enable innovation
- And, yes, protect the company when it all goes sideways

The best GCs are quietly powerful, deeply informed, and always a few steps ahead of the room.

If you master boardroom politics, drive business value, and play the CEO chess game right, you'll stop being "the lawyer" and start being the person no one wants to make a decision without.

And that's the endgame.

www.ingramcontent.com/pod-product-compliance
Lightning Source LLC
LaVergne TN
LVHW050922210926
848482LV00012B/499